A MISSING PIECE IN WELLNESS

# The Prevention of Depression

JOHN WEAVER, PSY.D.

**Outskirts Press, Inc.**
Denver, Colorado

Cover photo taken by John Weaver at Whitehaven Bed & Breakfast in Minocqua, Wisconsin.

*To my wife, Darlene, whose artist's soul continues to inspire me to grow and flourish in my work.*

# TABLE OF CONTENTS

I was attending the state convention of the Society of Human Resource Managers in Milwaukee, Wisconsin, during September of 2005. The speaker for one of the breakout sessions was talking about establishing wellness programs in the workplace, to reduce costs and increase the health of employees.

He identified the costs of a variety of illnesses. The most expensive cost (*70% higher than high blood glucose, which ranked second*) was depression. But his wellness program did not address depression.

I began to look to see who has addressed this important and expensive issue. I could not find any component of any wellness program that taught skills to prevent depression.

That is how my interest in psychological wellness was born. As a psychologist, I knew that we could design a program that would teach these skills. Psychologists have researched the prevention of depression, and many published studies demonstrate that these skills can be learned.

This book introduces you to these skills and gives you some ideas about how to apply them in your day-to-day life. The suggestions are not exhaustive. You can use the ideas presented here to spark your own ideas.

Please do not treat this only as a set of facts, though. As valuable as it is, *information does not lead to implementation*. If this information is going to be helpful to you, it is meant to lead you to take action. Practice some of the ideas and see where it leads.

# SIGNS OF DEPRESSION

*Every time history repeats itself,*
*the price goes up.*

*- Anonymous*

# SIGNS OF DEPRESSION

Do you have the following symptoms?

- *Depressed mood (such as feelings of sadness or emptiness)*
- *Reduced interest in activities that used to be enjoyed*
- *Sleep disturbances (either not being able to sleep well or sleeping too much)*
- *Loss of energy or a significant reduction in energy level*
- *Difficulty concentrating, holding a conversation, paying attention, or making decisions that used to be made fairly easily*
- *Suicidal thoughts or intentions (If you have suicidal thoughts, intentions or plans, **please consult a mental health professional immediately!**)*

Have you felt this way, more days than not, in the past two weeks? Are these feelings and thoughts interfering with your work or your life?

If so, you may have a depressive disorder.

Depression can be successfully treated with psychotherapy and medication. Talk to a psychologist or a mental health professional.

## The Course of Depression

The majority of individuals who have had an episode of depression will have a recurrence within five years, and those who have had more than one episode of depression in their lifetime are at increasing risk to have additional episodes.

The first episode of depression is usually triggered by a reaction to a stressful event. The response to this event, which is often sad or tragic, seems understandable to most people who hear about it.

> Depressive disorders are described as acute problems, but they often have a chronic course.

The second depressive episode seems to come a little quicker and a little easier. The event that seems to trigger the second depression does not need to be as intense. Others have a little less sympathy for the person this time. It can seem like an overreaction to life circumstances from the perspective of someone who has never been through a depression before.

The third (and subsequent depressions) can come with no clear precipitating event.

At this point the depressive feelings seem unpredictable. Family and friends cannot understand why it continues to happen. Some will suggest that it is due to a moral failing or lack of effort on the part of the person who is depressed. Professionals may suggest that the depression is due to a genetic predisposition or talk about an imbalance in the brain chemistry. The depression feels uncontrollable, which only adds to the sufferer's despair.

It is as if the experience of depression makes it easier and easier to get depressed. The threshold is lowered with each episode.

Depression is a chronic illness.

## Why Does Depression Happen?

It is important to clarify some things. When you are struggling with depression, the well-meaning attempts of family and friends, or even professionals, can leave you feeling helpless and hopeless about the disorder. Let's take a close

> There are three common ways of understanding depression:
> - As a *moral failing*
> - As a *genetic predisposition*
> - As a *chemical imbalance*
>
> Each explanation is inadequate on its own.

look at what some of these "labels" mean.

*Moral Failing.* When you are feeling depressed it can seem as if you are choosing to let yourself dwell on the negative in life. This perspective highlights the responsibility that you must assume for your own behavior.

It is true that when you become depressed, you tend to see the negative and overlook the positive dimensions in your life. You can wake up to a sunny day and find yourself dwelling on the rain forecast for later in the week.

Negative thinking about the past, the present, and the future is one of the characteristics of depression. When you are not depressed, negative thinking is not as prominent.

> Depression as a *moral failing* highlights the need to take responsibility for your own behavior, but it can leave you feeling you are to blame for your own suffering.

You are used to thinking that you can control what you think (although, in reality, it is much more complicated than that), so it seems that you should be able to make a decision to think positive thoughts to counter the depression.

The problem with holding the view that depression is a moral failing is that it not only describes the thoughts that you have when you are depressed, but it also casts blame on you when you are already suffering. While it is true that you must make an effort to change behavior to overcome patterns of depression, not all efforts will be equally effective. Depression is a complex reaction to circumstances. It takes skillful action to change.

Depression is not simply a moral failing, even if it is your responsibility to work for change.

*Genetic Predisposition.* Modern medicine has been very successful at identifying the genetic sources of many illnesses. This effort has

5

been helpful in guiding effective treatments and in the development of new medicines.

Depression as a *genetic predisposition* makes it clear that you may be susceptible to depression through no fault of your own, but you may then believe that there is nothing you can do to help yourself.

The term *genetic predisposition* is used to explain why you might have a particular reaction (i.e., contract a specific illness) and others will not, even in the same life circumstances. There are some individuals who more easily become depressed when encountering the difficult and tragic circumstances in life.

For others, the reaction may result in a strain on some other system in the body. Even if you are not predisposed to depression you may become depressed if the difficulties are severe or prolonged.

Unfortunately, the discussion that depression can be a "genetic predisposition" can also be interpreted as a reason to abdicate responsibility. After all, if you are "genetically programmed" to get this disease, or to act in this way, what can you do? For many the identification of a genetic contribution is taken to mean that there is nothing that can be done to prevent the illness from occurring.

Genes, however, are not your destiny!

Genes are better understood as biological habits that will express themselves unless you learn to break the habit and live more consciously.

***An Imbalance in Brain Chemistry.*** The pharmaceutical companies, in an attempt to help people understand the way that medicine alleviates the feelings of depression, use the phrase, "an imbalance in brain chemistry." The medicine is designed to assist the brain to restore a chemical level that will prompt feelings of happiness and pleasure.

What is often not understood, and is not well explained, is that your brain chemistry is constantly changing. It is changing as you read this sentence. Changes in brain chemistry occur as the brain receives signals from both outside and inside stimuli.

To say that you have an imbalance in your brain chemistry when you are depressed is an accurate statement. Levels of the brain chemical serotonin, and perhaps others, have changed. When this

> Depression as an *imbalance in brain chemistry* helps clarify why medicines can be effective in treatment, but you can change brain chemistry in other ways too, like using healthy thinking skills.

change occurs, the neurons themselves may become damaged, making it difficult for the brain to restore the chemicals to a proper balance.

We do not know if the changes in brain chemistry cause depression or if the changes are the result of depression. Restoring serotonin levels in the brain chemistry decreases the symptoms of depression and promotes healing of the neurons.

One way to alter that brain chemistry is with antidepressant medication; however, medication does not appear to decrease the risk of having another depressive episode unless you continue to take medication for the remainder of your life.

Brain changes also occur in response to cognitive therapy, but not as quickly as with medication, although with cognitive therapy, you may be more resistant to becoming depressed when future stressful situations arise.

*A Broader View.* Each of these contributions as to why depression happens gives you some insight into the disorder. When you feel depressed, you tend to see the negative and overlook the importance of the positive. You may be more prone to depression because of your genetics. When you are depressed, your brain chemistry also changes. These elements are all present during an episode of

7

depression, yet they do not adequately explain how depression becomes a chronic illness.

Within fifteen years of an episode of major depression, 80% of those who have been diagnosed will have had additional episodes.

The first episode almost always gets triggered by one of the difficult and tragic moments in life. Untreated, that depression will last between nine to eighteen months. With treatment, the length and intensity of the depression can be dramatically shortened.

The second episode, however, can usually be set in motion by an event that outside observers would think is less stressful, which may contribute to the impression that you seem particularly prone to depression.

You may have been exposed to something similar before your first episode and handled it without becoming depressed. After that first depression, though, a similar problem seems to be too much to handle. The event that triggered the depression may have been less intense, but your feelings of depression are just as painful as the first time.

The third (and subsequent) episodes of depression will seemingly arise with no external stress that precipitates it. You might wake up one morning feeling depressed. It no longer seems to be a reaction to the troubling events in life; the depression has taken on a life of its own.

When you were depressed the first time, you experienced the devastation that this disorder brings. You never wanted to feel that way again, so when the next event occurred (distressful events happen in everyone's life), you worried that you might become depressed again. Your worries caused you to become even more distressed in this situation. It quickly became a downward spiral of worry and distress that triggered the next depression.

The second depression proved to you that you could have new

episodes of depression at any time. It is a very troubling and worrisome thought, so the worry became your constant companion. The worry becomes a constant reminder to check, am I becoming depressed?

When your mood, which is always fluctuating, becomes sad, it can start the cycle that ends in another depressive episode. This time it does not need an external event, because you are already worried and watchful that depression can arise in reaction to something that is entirely internal.

While there are still many times, between periods of depression, when you are able to enjoy your life, new episodes seem to occur more easily. They become more distressing each time, and they occur more often.

You may begin to identify yourself as being depressed, rather than as someone who has a depressive disorder.

If this scenario describes you, or if you are worried that you may be headed in that direction in your life, then this book is for you.

# NOTES:

# TREATMENT OF DEPRESSION

*I've learned that when someone is looking sad, or says something
bad happened, never say,
"What's the matter?" or "What's wrong?"
Always say: "Do you want to talk about it?
I'm here for you."*

*- Age 14
From Live and Learn and Pass it On
VOL. IV*

# TREATMENT OF DEPRESSION

> *In this chapter, you will find information about methods for treating depression. This is not a substitute for the recommendations of a qualified mental health professional who is familiar with you and your unique circumstances.*

If you have been diagnosed with depression, you will benefit from treatment by a mental health professional.

The treatments for depression have been very successful in alleviating symptoms and improving quality of life; with most studies showing that approximately four out of five subjects reporting improvement from some form of treatment. According to scientific research, the most common and effective treatments are antidepressant medication and cognitive therapy.

**Antidepressant Medication**

The most frequently prescribed antidepressant medications are the selective serotonin reuptake inhibitors (SSRI). Prozac was the first (and best-known) of these medications, although there are many more of these types of medication available now. Each is similar in its basic mechanism of action, but the side effects will be different. Your doctor will help you to select the right one for you.

SSRI medications act by blocking the re-absorption of the brain chemical serotonin in the synaptic gap (a gap that is present between individual nerve cells in the brain).

Nerve cells communicate with each other in part by transmitting chemicals from one neuron to another. The chemical is released by one cell into the synaptic gap and picked up by another cell. This chemical process tells the new cell what to do. This explanation is, of course, a simplified way of explaining what occurs at the level of the individual cell.

> The most common type of antidepressant medication is known as an SSRI. There are other medications that may be appropriate for you, so consult with your physician and learn about options that are right for you.

When you feel depressed, the brain chemical serotonin is not being received by the new cell or is being received in amounts that are too small. As a result, the new cell does not activate, and you feel depressed.

The serotonin that is not taken up by the new cell is reabsorbed into the cell that originally released it into the gap.

The medication actually blocks that reabsorption (or reuptake) in the original cell, causing it to remain in the gap longer. This action gives the new cell a better chance of getting enough serotonin to be activated and to function normally.

If the cell's ability to receive serotonin has been damaged, the process of exposing the new cell to serotonin longer also facilitates healing in the cell.

***Delayed reaction.*** It is very important to understand that antidepressant medications are not immediately effective. It normally takes two to four weeks of daily medication doses for you to begin to notice

> Most antidepressant medication takes two to four weeks to begin to work. Take the medication exactly as your doctor recommends.

a change. The benefits of the medication should continue to reduce the symptoms of your depression, reaching maximum effectiveness after you have taken the medication for four to six weeks. Then you will continue to receive benefits for as long as you take the medication.

If you forget to take the medication consistently, or you become impatient and stop it too soon, it will be ineffective. Be sure to follow the directions of your doctor carefully so that the medication will help you to feel better as soon as possible.

*Side effects.* All medications have side effects. You may notice significant and troublesome side effects with one medication, whereas side effects may be barely noticeable with another.

Antidepressant medication is no different. There are side effects that are specific to each drug. Talk to your doctor and your pharmacist about what you should expect from your antidepressant.

When you receive a written list of side effects or you look at the list published by the pharmaceutical company, the most frequently reported side effect is listed first, and the list proceeds in descending order of occurrence. Side effects listed at the end of the list have a very low probability of happening to you.

*Who should prescribe?* According to a report published by the Department of Health and Human Services, a primary care physician first diagnosed 42% of those with major depression and 47% of those with generalized anxiety disorder. Unfortunately, according to the National Co-morbidity Survey Replication, only 12.7% of individuals treated in the general medical sector received minimally adequate care.

Any physician can prescribe, but if you believe you have a depressive disorder, or if you have been diagnosed with one, a psychiatrist is the specialist in antidepressant medication. Psychiatrists will be familiar with the broad array of options to provide the best medication for your treatment.

## Cognitive Therapy

Research has shown that cognitive therapy is equally as effective as antidepressant medication in the treatment of depression. Cognitive therapy is a particular type of psychotherapy (talk therapy) that teaches you how to change the negative thinking patterns that arise when you have a depressive disorder.

Your thinking patterns change when you are in a depressed mood, as if you see the world through a dark lens. You magnify negative events and minimize the positive. You are likely to find yourself remembering

> Cognitive therapy requires that you actively participate with your therapist. You may choose to take medication and learn cognitive therapy skills at the same time.

the past hurts you have endured and see the future as a never-ending pattern of defeat. It seems as if it is "all or nothing," and since you can see flaws even in good things, it appears as if everything is spoiled.

This is not the way you think when you are not feeling depressed. Your thinking changes as your mood changes. When you are in a happy mood, you see the future as full of opportunities, but when you are in a depressed mood, the same future looks bleak.

Cognitive therapy is a treatment that helps you identify the thoughts that are arising from your current feeling state. You will learn ways of testing those thoughts so that you can identify which ones are not only negative but also unrealistic.

By challenging those thoughts, you can begin to challenge the depressed mood that is associated with those thoughts. *And changing your thoughts begins to change the chemistry of your brain!*

*How it works.* You learn the strategies of cognitive therapy by working with your therapist. Your therapist might be a psychologist, clinical social worker, licensed professional counselor, or other mental health professional. Cognitive therapy is a particular type of therapy, so ask your mental health professional if he or she is trained in this approach.

You begin by learning to notice your "automatic thoughts." These are thoughts that take place almost as a running commentary in your head, interpreting your experience. You can probably notice that you are having thoughts that provide you with an interpretation of reading these words right now.

You might be thinking, "That's very interesting," or "I don't have automatic thoughts!"

By noticing the ongoing commentary, you will be able to see that many of these thoughts match your mood and that they in fact are more reflective of your mood than of the reality of life going on around you. It is as if your mood is a blindfold preventing you from seeing life as it actually is.

The goal of cognitive therapy is not to teach you to be always positive, but to realistically assess your self and the world in which you live.

When you feel depressed, you judge things to be more negative than they actually are, and you begin to believe that your abilities are not sufficient to meet the mood-colored situations you are seeing.

You learn, in this therapy, to systematically evaluate the truth of your own thinking and discover ways to think thoughts that reflect reality more accurately. This facilitates your efforts to change your thoughts to be more successful in resisting the effects of feeling depressed.

***Side effects.*** Compared to antidepressant medication, cognitive therapy is equally effective in the treatment of depression, but it works differently from drug therapy.

In cognitive therapy, you identify, assess, and challenge thought patterns, which only indirectly changes moods, so it will take longer for you to feel better with cognitive therapy than it will if you use medications.

It takes effort to learn to change the way you think, so individuals who are feeling severely depressed or who have very low energy may need medication to alleviate the symptoms enough to be able to use the cognitive strategies you will be taught.

There are other talk therapies that are effective in treating depression. Ask your therapist about what approach will be best for you.

Unlike drug therapy, however, there is a much better chance that you will be resistant to future episodes of depression when you can learn and apply the lessons of cognitive therapy.

Other talk therapies may also be effective in successfully treating depression, including mindfulness-based cognitive therapy, interpersonal therapy, acceptance and commitment therapy, and dialectical behavioral therapy, among others.

Many people decide to take medication *and* learn the skills taught by cognitive therapy. This combination is certainly an option you should consider if you have been diagnosed with depression.

# NOTES:

# VALUE OF PREVENTION

*What we do today, right now,*
*Will have an accumulated effect*
*on all our tomorrows.*

*- Alexandra Stoddard*

Depression is expensive. When health insurance companies break down the prices of illnesses, the most costly is depression. It is more costly by almost twice the next most-expensive illness, which is high blood glucose (diabetes). Depression is even more costly to your company, because it causes more frequent absences from work, higher rates of disability, and lower performance at work.

The current approach to treating depression and other mental illnesses is very costly, too. When you are diagnosed with depression, you are referred to a very expensive doctor who will meet with you one on one. He or she will either

> Prevention is more effective than treatment. It costs less, and it improves the quality of your life experience.

prescribe medication you will take for a very long time, or you will meet with a psychologist or other therapist, again one on one, perhaps for six months or more.

The expense and length of treatment matters, because you are paying for the rising health insurance premiums through lower wages or cuts in other benefits. According to the Kaiser Foundation, the cost of health insurance rose 73% between the years 2000 and 2005. It has continued to rise four times faster than wages between 2005 and 2009.

Depression is also expensive in another way. It erodes the quality of life of the depressed individual. If you work hard to obtain financial security and create a home for your family but you can't enjoy it because you are caught in the web of depression, what have you gained?

Healthy thinking, therefore, is valuable, because of reduced expenses and improved quality of life.

23

Healthy thinking skills:
- Mindfulness
- Optimism
- Resilience

Healthy thinking involves learning skills associated with *mindfulness, optimism,* and *resilience.* These ways of thinking have been shown in research to raise your resistance to being diagnosed with a depressive disorder and to assist you in recovering more quickly if you go through a period with a depressed mood. In addition, healthy-thinking skills add to your happiness.

*Mindfulness.* Imagine that you have left work, driven home, and realized that you arrived in your driveway with no clear memories of how you got there. You were thinking about a problem you encountered before you left or you were anticipating some situation at home, and your driving took place on "automatic pilot."

Much of life goes by without notice while you are caught up in thoughts about something else. Mindless living can become a problem when it causes you to react to feelings of depression without thinking.

Mindfulness is a way of paying attention in a particular way: on purpose, in the present moment, and non-judgmentally. It teaches you to be more aware of decisions you can make

The goal of mindfulness is awareness, not relaxation.

to respond skillfully to the distress in your life. When you are mindful, you are able to bring all your abilities and talents to resolving the issues that arise in your life.

Mindfulness skills have been shown in research to reduce the relapse rates of depression by one-half. Up to 40% of those who learned mindfulness skills have been able to eliminate antidepressant medication without additional episodes of depression.

The research suggests that mindfulness skills are more helpful for those who have had three or more episodes of depression. It is an effective, non-pharmaceutical way to manage chronic depression.

*Optimism.* If you are pessimistic, you are probably more realistic about the odds you will be successful in your life, but if you are optimistic, you will probably beat those odds. When you are optimistic, you are more successful at preventing depression because you have developed a strategy for life that is extraordinarily effective.

Optimism is not simply positive thinking. When you advocate believing that everything is going to work out (positive thinking) no matter how the situation appears, you are less likely to be successful in the long run. Eventually, your prediction proves to be incorrect, which is emotionally devastating. And when you have employed positive thinking but the outcome is not positive, it is easy to blame yourself for the failure.

If, instead, you are an optimist, you believe in the value of effort. When you are confronted by difficult circumstances, you are eager to learn and grow from the challenge ahead. You believe in your talents and abilities.

> The skill of optimism is associated with success.

Because you approach difficult tasks as an opportunity to learn rather than seeing it as a need to prove yourself, you become skilled in new abilities. When you succeed at a task, you want to apply what you have learned in other, similar and not-so-similar situations.

And if a skill or strategy works once, it seems probable that it will continue to work in the future. Because you continue to apply your successful actions to new situations, you increase the chances of finding new places that your efforts will succeed.

*Resilience.* What are some of the hard things in life from which you have had to bounce back? Success in life is not dependent on avoiding the hard things in life but in having the resilience to meet the challenges.

You develop resilience by practicing several specific basic skills. You identify what is most important in your life, meet the challenges that arise rather than avoid them, and identify what is in your control and what it not.

When you suffer through hard times, the meaning that you assign to the difficulties makes a difference in how you cope. If you see the efforts you are making to deal with the stress as having

> Resilience is a tool for dealing with the tough parts of real life.

value to your family, having a spiritual purpose, or even as a means of personal growth, you will be more resilient.

If you are able to view the issue as an interesting challenge rather than yet another problem, you will be more inclined to work harder and even enjoy the efforts you are making.

When you are most effective at meeting the challenges of difficult times, you are able to focus on the part of what you can do that is in your control and let go of those aspects of the situation not in your control.

***Motivation for prevention.*** You probably don't need to be convinced of the value of prevention...at least not in theory. You know that your car needs regular maintenance and your home needs attention so that these important commodities will function properly.

You know that your body needs regular maintenance too. You should eat healthy foods and get regular exercise. Annual physicals and control of weight and blood pressure all make sense.

Most people have heard about the need to prevent problems, yet few engage in preventive behaviors.

If you are like the average person, you react to something that is in pain, but you will not engage in prevention as an automatic response. Why is it so difficult to practice prevention?

Human beings are *not* set up to notice what is *not* there.

This grammatically troublesome sentence with a double negative is intentional. It points to the most difficult challenge you face in shifting to a preventive approach to life.

When you are in pain, you notice it and do something about it. But after sitting for an hour at a meeting, how aware are you of the parts of your body that feel good?

This effect actually appears to be grounded in your instinct for survival. If you are walking in the desert and come up to an oasis with a beautiful pool of water, colorful flowers, a couple of shady palm trees, and just one lion, what is going to catch your attention? If you don't pay attention to the lion, even though everything else is much more pleasant, you will be eaten, and you won't have any children.

You are the descendant of parents who paid attention to the lion.

If you work hard on controlling your weight and staying fit and healthy, what do you get? Nothing! You don't get a heart attack or diabetes. Because you are like the average person, you don't notice what isn't there, so why go through all the trouble to be well?

> To be effective at staying healthy, define your goals in positive terms rather than negative ones.

You do react to something that is in pain, but you will not engage in prevention as an automatic response. It will occur only if you are consciously choosing to do something that is preventive.

It is actually harder than that! You know that the most difficult thing about exercise is that it is not pleasant to do it. Healthy food does not taste the same as food dripping with fat and calories. Likewise, learning healthy thinking skills–to be mindful, resilient, and optimistic–takes effort. The benefit comes only after the work.

It is very important to understand this fact. You will not keep up an exercise routine if you need to feel good all the while you exercise.

27

You must also learn to ignore the negative thoughts that pop up while you tune into the skills of being mindful, optimistic, and resilient.

It feels good when you have done the work of taking care of yourself. Too often, you are so busy that you might overlook those pleasant feelings and therefore overlook a potential source of inspiration to make healthy choices. Paying attention, on purpose, to the way it feels when you are taking good care of your health is an important motivator that will keep you working at doing things that are preventive.

## How to Use the Remainder of This Book

The rest of this book contains ninety tips for putting the skills of mindfulness, optimism, and resilience into practice in your daily life. When you read them, you might be overwhelmed by the realization that you cannot practice all these suggestions, at least not all at once!

If your depressive thinking kicks in, you might then feel like a failure because you will not meet your internal expectations and your beliefs about what you "should" be doing. That's just your depression talking, so try not to pay any attention to it.

Instead, accept these tips in the spirit in which they are being offered to you, as suggestions. Here are a few ideas about how to approach the section.

1. You might take a single section (for example, you could select the "on purpose" dimension of Mindfulness) and see what suggestions you could apply. Later you might decide to try a different suggestion, perhaps from the Optimism or the Resilience chapter.

2. You could pick a tip each day. You would have ninety days of practical ideas that you could put into your thoughts and actions, to develop healthy thinking skills.

3. If you find your favorites, the ones you are already practicing, you can add to your healthy thinking with tips that are similar.

There are many ways to use these suggestions, so be creative and become healthier in the process.

# MINDFULNESS

*"To affect the quality of the day,
that is the highest of arts."*

- *Ralph Waldo Emerson*

# MINDFULNESS

The origins of mindfulness are thousands of years old. Every major spiritual tradition has developed methods for increasing mindful living. More recently, psychologists Jon Kabat-Zinn, Richard Davidson, and Zindel Segal, among others, have begun to use these methods to address physical and psychological health issues.

Brain imaging studies have revealed that people who practice mindfulness are able to develop the regions of the brain that are responsible for happiness and feelings of peacefulness, while the areas that are associated with depression, fear, and anger begin to weaken.

Mindfulness decreases the risk of becoming depressed by 50%, but it also has been applied in various endeavors to increase performance.

NBA coach Phil Jackson attributes the success of his world-champion Chicago Bulls and Los Angeles Lakers teams, at least in part, to the mindfulness skills he taught and practiced with these professional athletes. Mindfulness skills added a unique benefit that the other NBA athletes did not possess.

Being able to pay attention

...on purpose
...in the present moment
...with a non-judgmental attitude

provides you with tools to handle a range of human experience.

# ON PURPOSE

Dolly Parton once said, "Our job is to find out who we are, and do it intentionally!" When you live your life on purpose, you are no longer a victim of your circumstances. You choose how to respond to the events in your life. You are no longer missing what is happening because you are on "automatic pilot," and you become and actor rather than a reactor.

*1. Whenever you eat or drink something, take a minute and breathe. Bring awareness to seeing your food, smelling your food, tasting your food, chewing your food, and swallowing your food.*

There is a reason "fast food" is called "fast food." It is meant to be eaten while you are hurrying from one part of your life to the next. You are not paying attention to the taste of the food, but are focused on driving, or preparing for the next meeting, or mentally engaging in some other activity. If you stopped and paid attention to the taste of the food, you would notice it is heavy in salt and fat content.

When your ancestors ate on the run, it was because they were probably fleeing from some danger–a battle, a predator, or a natural disaster–and they needed food that would be packed with calories for an uncertain journey. As a result, the taste for foods with high fat or salt became a meal that was attractive during times of stress.

Healthful food tends to have a more delicate taste. It is best eaten in an environment that promotes savoring each bite and enjoying the experience.

*2. Notice your initial reaction to events in your life. Make the choice to respond out of your values rather than your reactions.*

You may have heard the saying that "On your deathbed, you won't wish you spent more time at the office."

This saying is powerful because it causes you to stop and put things into a larger perspective. Making the choice to conclude one more business deal is not really as important as the time spent with a family member. It is not really so critical to make the meeting on time that you overlook the tears of your small child who wants to tell you an important "secret."

You know your values. You know what is important in life, but it takes effort to stop and see a small event in a larger context, so you can make a decision that will foster what you really hold to be true in your life.

Mindful awareness invites you to step back from the pressure of the moment and see the bigger picture of your life today. Don't wait until you are on your deathbed to understand what is really important in your life.

*3. Make yourself aware of how each day is a new opportunity to live as you intend. You may have reacted to something in a particular way in the past, but you still have a choice about how you want to be now.*

You probably have routines and patterns that guide your life, if you are normal. These routines help you make sense of your world and respond in predictable and consistent ways. You build them through the past experiences and you now "know" how to relate to situations in which you find yourself in the present.

Like many good things, you can overdo the predictability of your responses to life. For example, you might react to someone you love because of something he or she did that reminds you of an action that hurt you in the past.

As best you can, try to mindfully pay attention to other possible ways to respond to things that happen in your life. Sometimes the best choices will not be the decisions that were effective in the past. You have the power to choose differently in each situation.

*4. Focus your attention on your daily activities, such as brushing your teeth, taking a shower, making a meal, putting on your coat, or doing your job. Bring mindfulness to each activity.*

Think about taking a walk with a three-year-old child. She will not walk like an adult walker. She will stop to look at stones, leaves, and piles of dirt and be fascinated by the most mundane things. She is also having a lot more fun than adults taking the same walk!

There is hidden value in the ordinary activities of your life. Many moments that seem ordinary may offer the possibility for discovery of something fascinating, even important.

It is important to cultivate an appreciation for the ordinary tasks of life. By paying attention, on purpose, you will be open for the possibilities to learn, grow, and experience joy in even the simple things.

*5. Learn that you can stay with your intention even when it is difficult. Discomfort or distress can be challenging, but they do not have to derail you from your purpose.*

Think about someone you consider a hero. It could be a figure from history or someone you know and admire in your life. Think about what makes that person heroic to you.

She is not a hero because everything in her life went smoothly and always worked out for the best. You see her as heroic because of choices that showed courage or compassion or wisdom in the midst of difficult circumstances. Her ability to make a good choice in the face of adversity is the quality you admire.

The circumstances of your life do not define who you are. The choices you make during difficult times shape your life and provide you with the chance that you could be a heroic figure for someone else. Life will bring distress and pain into your experience, as it does in everyone's life. The heroic thing to do is to continue to be the best person you can be, even in trying times.

*6. When you are distracted from your intention, as soon as you notice, make the decision to gently but firmly bring your attention back to your purpose. It is the nature of the mind to wander, but making the decision to continually bring it back trains it to become more focused.*

When people are first introduced to mindful meditation, it is a universal reaction to think, "I can't do this! My mind keeps wandering! Even though I want to keep my mind calm and focused, it keeps being distracted."

This is a normal experience. It describes a normal mind.

The purpose of learning to be mindful is to become *more aware*, not to develop a tool to escape from your life. Your mind thinks about a multitude of things during every waking moment. It often is thinking about something that is not relevant to the moment at hand.

When you need to keep your focus, it is most effective to observe your mind. As soon as you notice it is thinking about something other than what you intended, guide it back to your intention.

*7. When your wants are in conflict with your values, notice that you are able to make a choice to live in accord with your values, even if it means letting go of some temporary pleasant experience or embracing a painful one.*

Sometimes the saying "live for the moment" is interpreted to mean that you should just do what is pleasurable in life without regard to your values or your future, but this is not a way to gain satisfaction in your life. Satisfaction arises from choosing to live in accord with your values, even when it is a challenge to do so.

You have done hard things in your life before. You have been willing to endure something that was painful or uncomfortable because you were working for something that was valuable. You might have been training for a sport, learning a musical instrument, or creating a piece of art.

All things that are valuable require some effort to achieve. "In the moment" you understand that letting go of some pleasure or embracing some pain is a choice to endure some temporary hardship in the service of moving toward something more significant in your life.

*8. Practice letting go of what just happened so that you can bring your awareness into the situation at hand. Your life is constantly changing, and you need to be paying attention to make good decisions right now.*

You can practice letting go of the past and moving on to the next moment by taking a moment and observing your breath. Watch your exhale with particular attention. Make sure you release all the air from your lungs.

The next breath happens automatically. In fact, you are not ready for the next breath until you let go of the previous one. As vital and necessary as it is to breathe in, it is just as vital and necessary to breathe out.

This fact is parallel to your life. You must let go of what just happened, in order to be ready to be fully engaged in what is happening in this moment.

You can practice this important life skill by attending to your breathing, starting by noticing the outbreath first and observing several breaths through the full cycle.

*9. There is a saying, "When the student is ready, the teacher will arrive." What is the situation in your life right now that offers you an opportunity to learn and to grow?*

When you are deeply engaged in wishful thinking, you may be missing the opportunity to learn and grow from the circumstances in your life as they exist right now.

Your child is having a tantrum about something that seems really small to you. What can you learn from this situation that will make you a better person?

You are having trouble with a coworker who is making unreasonable demands. Is there a way you need to change and grow to be able to handle this stressful environment better?

By treating the challenges of your life as opportunities, you will discover new ways to see things and new ways to live in accord with your best self.

*10. Be patient with yourself. Learning to live your life on purpose will take time. You are not failing just because you notice that this is difficult.*

The world around us is filled with messages of "instant gratification." You can get immediate updates from your television, your computer, and even your phone. You can make instant meals. Fast travel routes are publicized so you won't get stuck in a traffic jam.

But many things that are valuable in life still take time to develop. You will get better at what you practice. You don't have to expect that you will be an instant expert at being mindful. You can learn and grow throughout your life and continue to become more effective at living your life "on purpose."

What other ways have you thought about that would help you to live your life "on purpose?"

_____

_____

_____

_____

_____

What was your favorite tip for living your life "on purpose?"

_____

_____

What will you do today to live "on purpose?"

_____

_____

# IN THE PRESENT MOMENT

Everything in your life takes place in the present moment. You can remember the past or plan for the future, but events happen in the here and now.

*1. When you first wake up in the morning, before you get out of bed, bring your attention to your breathing. Notice as you make a transition from one posture to the next. Take three "mindful" breaths.*

Your mindset is important. When **you** wake up in the morning, you might find yourself thinking anxious, angry, or depressed thoughts, and these thoughts can set a tone for the day.

Try bringing your mind to a more mindful place as soon as you are able. You don't need to resolve all the issues and problems that come up in the turmoil of emotions at this moment. You probably cannot resolve them right now. The troubles of the day will confront you soon enough. But they are not here now. You do not need to start worrying about them now.

Instead, make the choice to connect to this moment. Breathe. Move. Let this be the place to start your day.

*2. Whenever you hear a phone ring, a bird sing, a train pass by, laughter, a car horn, the wind, the sound of a door closing, or any other sound, use that sound as the bell of mindfulness. Really listen and be present and awake.*

It can be difficult to stay in the present moment, so most major spiritual traditions have devised ways to break into the day-to-day responsibilities with a call to prayer.

In the tradition of medieval Europe, churches remind Christians to engage in prayer by sounding the church bells at 6:00 A.M., noon, and 6:00 P.M. In the Islamic tradition there is a call to prayer five times a day. Buddhists use prayer wheels to remind the faithful to stay in touch with meditation.

You can find your own way of calling your attention back to being in a "mindful" state. Pick a particular sound to be a reminder. It is best if the sound is frequent but not constant, so that it will be easier to notice it.

Each time you hear the sound, take a "mindful" breath and notice what is happening in the moment. Make choices about how you want to be in this particular set of circumstances.

*3. Be aware of any points of tightness in your body throughout the day. See if you can breathe into them and, as you exhale, let go of excess tension. Is there tension stored anywhere in your body? For example: your neck, shoulders, stomach, jaw, or lower back?*

Your body is giving you information about what is going on in the present moment. Those points of excess tension alert you to the presence of stress or to the presence of some other physical concern.

You might choose to try to ignore the discomfort or to take a pain reliever to rid yourself of it, but an alternative is to take a few moments to acknowledge your bodily sensation. Be curious about what it is telling you about this moment. Then breathe into it, rather than distract yourself. As you let go of the breath, imagine yourself letting go of the tension at the same time.

You might notice that tension is likely to show up in a particular region of your body. As you get to know yourself, you will be better at identifying the physical signs and addressing the emotions associated with stresses in your life.

*4. When you have worrisome thoughts about a future event, remind yourself that the event has not yet happened (and may never happen) and bring your thoughts back to what you are doing right now.*

Worry is an interesting thing. When you worry about a future event, it is as if you are placing yourself in that event right now, as you worry, and you begin to imagine how you will deal with it.

Later you might find that the event you worried about never happened. You worried about it and reacted to it as if it were happening, but it was unnecessary, because it was not a real worry.

Or you may find that it does happen. Now you have to experience the event a second time–the first time was during the time when you were worried. If it is an unpleasant event, then you have had to go through the unpleasantness twice.

Either way, the worry has added to your distress rather than helped you live more successfully.

*5. Notice the pleasant sensations in your body right now. Then notice the neutral sensations. It is easy to get caught up in discomfort, but there is much more going on in the moment.*

It is easy to notice pain and discomfort. When something is distressing, it breaks through your consciousness and intrudes on what you are doing.

Pleasant events do not do this. You must make a choice to notice something that is pleasant. It is easy to overlook what is going well.

The conscious awareness of a pleasant event is part of the enjoyment of it. Make an attempt to bring these events into your awareness on a regular basis.

*6. Try to see the world through the eyes of a small child. Be aware of the wonder of children and appreciate seeing something as if it were for the first time.*

When my oldest grandson was about one and a half years old, he and his parents were at my house during the first snowfall of the season. The adults were gathered at our dining room table, and we were looking out at the snow and grumbling about the long winter, when he came into the room.

He had never seen snow before, that he remembered, so he stopped right in his tracks, his eyes got big, and he said, "Wow! Look!"

He proceeded to take each one of us, individually, by the hand, led us to the patio door, and showed us the snow.

I saw the snow through his eyes that day, and each year, during the first snowfall I remember what he did and try to see the snow through those eyes again.

What has a small child taught you about how to see your world?

*7. Recognize that each moment is constantly changing. You may be in distress right now. When the next moment comes, it offers new possibilities that can occur only in that new moment. The suffering (and the pleasure) of this moment is temporary.*

Monks from a Buddhist tradition construct elaborate works of art made of individual grains of colored sand. These sand paintings, which take hours to complete, are done outside where the wind quickly blows them away.

The monks explain that they engage in this process to remind themselves of the fleeting, changeable nature of life.

You will have times in life that are painful and difficult. You will experience distress. It is difficult, during these times, to remember that it is temporary. Dark days pass, and new days come with new possibilities. Treat this time as it really is, a set of circumstances that will change. Life is always changing.

*8. Try to live each moment as if it were the only moment like that one that you will ever have. It is. You are alive for a limited time, so it is important to make each moment count.*

It can seem as if the important times in life are few and far between. It can seem as if you are spending your life waiting for the significant events to occur.

But this is the only time in your whole life that you will experience a moment quite like this one. One Zen saying reminds the listener, "You cannot step in the same river twice." The river is always changing and you are always changing.

If you need to tell someone you love him or her, don't wait until tomorrow; do it now. If you need to appreciate the environment you are in, do it now. If you need to become a better person, now is the time to begin. This is the most important moment you have right now.

*9. Resist the impulse to distract yourself from the discomfort in this moment. If there is discomfort in your life, you need all of your attention to make skillful decisions about how to respond.*

Recent scientific studies with chronic pain patients have uncovered a surprising result. When pain patients try to distract themselves from pain by trying to focus on something more pleasant or engrossing, the long-term outcome is an increase in the experience of pain. It is more successful to purposefully pay attention to the pain and try to observe it non-judgmentally.

You might try doing the same thing, in a moment of discomfort. Focus on it. Treat it as an experiment.

Approach the dimension of your life that is unpleasant and observe it carefully. As best you can, be curious about the experience rather than give in to the urge to wish it would go away. See what you can learn from approaching it in this way.

If you notice that it helps, try it again. If not, you can try something else the next time.

*10. Use your senses to bring you back into the moment. What are you seeing? Hearing? Smelling? Tasting?*

Notice the visual images you can see as you look up from this book. See the colors, shapes, and shadows.

Notice the sounds that reach your ears right now. Let go of labeling what the sounds are, but listen to the tone and rhythm of the sensation. Those sounds have been present all along but are only now in your consciousness.

Notice the fragrances in the air as you pay close attention to what you can smell. If you smell nothing, notice that you smell nothing.

What is the taste in your mouth? Can you still taste food you recently ate? Is the sensation stronger on one part of your tongue than another part?

Notice what you are touching right now. This might include a sensation of your back against the seat or how your clothes contact your skin.

These five senses lead you back to awareness of the experience in this moment. Pay attention to "now."

What other ways have you thought about that would help you to live your life "in the present moment?"

_____

_____

_____

_____

_____

What was your favorite tip for living your life "in the present moment?"

_____

_____

What will you do today to live "in the present moment?"

_____

_____

# WITH A NON-JUDGMENTAL ATTITUDE

Georgia O'Keefe, the painter, said, "All of my life I have been afraid, and I never let it keep me from doing anything I wanted to do." Your life is filled with pleasant and unpleasant events. You have successes and failures. This is neither because you are inadequate nor because you are extraordinary. It is because you are human.

*1. Practice being grateful for your life, even if it is not what you want it to be. Both good things and bad things happen all the time, and you can choose to be grateful for many things every day.*

It is easy to be grateful for the pleasant things in your life, and it is important to do so. Take a moment to bring to mind two things in your life that are pleasant. Be thankful for them.

It is more difficult to be grateful for difficult things in your life. The painful part of life is an opportunity to learn and to grow. While you may not be grateful for the pain, you can be thankful that you have an opportunity to choose to live your life in a way that has value and integrity.

Practicing gratitude is a way to practice being open to the lessons of life, and it makes you happier and more joyful about your daily existence.

*2. Bring awareness to listening and talking. Listen without agreeing or disagreeing or planning what you will say when it is your turn. When talking, try to say just what you need to say without overstating or understating.*

Listening is a skill that must be developed. Many people are so worried about what they need to say that they don't even hear what the other person is saying.

Practice your listening skills by trying to listen without judging the "rightness" or "wrongness" of the speaker. After the speaker stops speaking, take a mindful breath and respond from your heart.

You don't need to plan out what you say. Instead, say what you believe to be true. It can be said without making any emphasis that dramatizes your point. Be straightforward in your speech.

*3. Notice your thoughts and your reactions without evaluating them. Accept your inner thoughts and recognize that reality is often different from your thoughts about reality.*

Sometimes, if you are normal, you will notice that you are thinking thoughts that you would not want to repeat to another person.

It is not necessary to act on these thoughts, but before you make an attempt to exclude them from your consciousness, take a moment and do your best to be curious.

What is that thought? What does it say about my current emotions? What am I experiencing right now that may give rise to this way of thinking?

Remember, you have thoughts, but you are not identified with your thoughts. They come and go. You do not need to believe everything you think!

4. *Accept the circumstances of your life right now. They are whatever they are. To move forward, you must make your choices based on what is really going on, rather than wishing it were otherwise.*

If you are walking through the woods and there is a bear hiding behind a tree around the bend, would it be better to know that the bear is there or not to know?

Some people live as if they do not want to know details about their own life. It is certainly less distressing in the short run to ignore the dangers that lie ahead and keep behaving as if everything will work out for the best., but when the dangers, like the bear, are real, it is wise to be paying attention, so you can make your best decisions.

Mindfulness does not guarantee that life will always be smooth; it gives you skills to live in the best way possible in the midst of this life you have.

*5. Notice an area of your body that is itching. Rather than scratching, just observe it for a while. The itch becomes more intense but then changes or goes away. So do many discomforts in life.*

Itching sensations are quite common. If you sit very still for a brief period of time, you will notice some area of your body that itches.

This time, try to just observe the itch. In your mind's eye, enter into the experience of the itch and watch what is happening.

It may intensify as you initially notice it. It may even seem like it is too hard not to scratch it. Try to accept that the impulse to scratch is just an impulse. Keep watching without scratching, if you can.

You may notice that the itch starts to feel less intense as you watch it. It may finally go away on its own, although it will pop up again in a different area of the body. It is not necessary to do anything to make the itching go away; this process happens naturally.

*6. Commit yourself to learn something from the difficulties you endure. Although you will experience bad things in your life, you can still learn from them.*

To hold that you can learn from the pain and tragedy in life is not the same as believing that a bad thing is really a good thing in disguise. It is recognition that you have a strength inside, one that you might not fully appreciate, which will guide you through difficult times, if you let it.

Bad things don't happen as a punishment for being a bad person. Bad things happen to everyone at sometime in life.

You are still able to choose what kind of person you want to be, even when things are hard. When you recognize that choice, you have the opportunity to grow, no matter what your life circumstances.

*7. Think of someone who loves you. Cultivate an accepting attitude of loving actions toward you. Even when those actions are not exactly what you want, accept them in the spirit in which they were performed.*

Have you ever given one of your friends a compliment and noticed that he or she dismissed it? This kind of "humility" diminishes you and makes it hard for your friend to appreciate the strengths you have seen in him or her.

Do you dismiss the compliments others give to you?

Greet the kindness of others with a simple, "Thank you." As best you can, accept the loving actions directed toward you as authentic and valuable. Even if the actions are not exactly what you wish they would be, be willing to see them as gestures of love.

*8. Think of someone who has hurt you. Recognize that you remain capable of choosing your response, even in the face of the pain they caused.*

It is easy to nurture the impulse to want to hurt someone who has hurt you. You feel justified in being angry and you want to get even. But all the while you are harboring feelings of anger, you are also experiencing the distress that goes along with those thoughts, and the person who has hurt you is not even aware of most of what you are experiencing.

The anger you are holding is affecting the quality of your life in a negative way.

You can choose (this *is* a hard choice to make) to respond differently to this hurt.

Instead of giving in to anger and wishing to return hurt for hurt, you can work to maintain your inner sense of peace and calm, not because it is acceptable to be hurt by another person but because it is not acceptable to you to be changed by that hurt.

*9. Feelings of sadness or worry are normal and do not mean that you will develop a mental disorder.*

If you are mindful of your inner emotional states, you will notice that there are times when you will feel sad or worried about something in your life.

If you have had a depressive episode in the past, or you have been prone to worry, you may be concerned that you are falling back into a state of mental dis-ease.

Feelings of sadness and worry are a normal part of being human. Acknowledge the feelings, and even let yourself become more aware of what is happening, letting go of judgment about it as you do so.

Notice the rhythms of emotion. Sadness dominates for a period of time, but then gives way to new emotional sensations like hopefulness or love. It is only if sadness or worry become "stuck" and interfere with your ability to function in daily life that you should be concerned. If you are stuck in a negative emotion, consult with a mental health professional.

*10. Accept that you will sometimes be judgmental. As soon as you notice, let the judgment go.*

Trying not to be judgmental is very difficult. You notice that you have fallen into judgment, and then you begin to judge yourself for being judgmental. You can even find yourself judging yourself for judging yourself for being judgmental!

You will sometimes find that judgments arise in the course of being mindfully aware of your life. When it happens, remember that it is a common experience.

Rather than getting upset, accept it as a part of life and simply let it go.

What other ways have you thought about that would help you live your life with a non-judgmental attitude?

_____

_____

_____

_____

_____

What was your favorite tip for living your life with a non-judgmental attitude?

_____

_____

What will you do today to live with a non-judgmental attitude?

_____

_____

# OPTIMISM

*When you follow your bliss...doors will open where you would not have thought there would be doors; and where there wouldn't be a door for anyone else.*

*- Joseph Campbell*

# OPTIMISM

When Martin Seligman was elected president of the American Psychological Association, he announced that he wanted to introduce an initiative to research positive psychology. The scientific endeavors of psychologists have always been oriented toward understanding human behavior, but since World War II, the emphasis has been increasingly directed toward understanding the behavior that underlie the diseases of humans.

Dr. Seligman, along with other researchers based at the University of Pennsylvania and some at the University of Wisconsin, had already begun to focus on optimism.

Optimism is not just positive thinking. Optimism is grounded in a way of understanding what importance you assign to your own actions. This understanding is roughly divided into three dimensions:

    personal,
    permanent, and
    pervasive.

If you are an optimist you believe that when something good happens it is due (at least in part) to your personal efforts. Pessimists believe they are personally responsible for bad things. As an optimist you believe that the good things in your life can be permanent, and that those good things will be found pervasively. Pessimists see bad things as lasting and occurring throughout their life.

If you develop the skills of optimism, you are less likely to become depressed, even if the circumstances of your life are difficult.

"I have learned from experience that the greater part of our happiness or misery depends on our dispositions and not on our circumstances." This quote from Martha Washington captures the essence of the mindset that you acquire when you approach life optimistically.

*1. Acknowledge your talents and abilities. Notice that you are good at some things. Learn to cherish your own unique gifts.*

If you know what you do well, you can make choices to use your talents and abilities in the way you live your life. Take a moment and notice what those gifts are.

Set aside any impulse you might have to be humble during this exercise. You don't have to proclaim your strengths to the whole world, but you do need to know what they are for yourself.

You will be more successful in your life if you are able to focus your energy on the elements in your life where you do well. You will notice both strengths and weaknesses, but you will be able to be a high performer by developing the talents that you have.

*2. Take something you enjoy doing and learn more about it. You will enjoy it even more when you acquire knowledge about it and skill at doing it.*

Imagine that you are the manager of a small office. You have a limited budget for training, and as you look around the office you know that you can send each person for a developmental seminar.

How should you make the decision about which person to send to which seminar?

For example, your office manager is a good communicator, but she is weak on organization. If you choose to send her to a seminar to rectify her weakness, she would become better organized, but would do it only reluctantly. It is not something she finds easy to do.

But if you send her to develop her communication skills, she will be enthusiastic about being the best communicator she can be. As an outstanding communicator, she will be able to let others in the office–like someone who loves organizing–fill the roles that she does not do as well.

The same is true for you. You develop your talents to the highest degree by learning as much as you can about what you naturally do well.

*3. When you perform a task and it goes well, identify the actions you took that contributed to the positive outcome. Acknowledge that your actions were important in obtaining the final results.*

Think of a time when you were successful in your life. What did you do that contributed to that success? Can you identify the key actions and attitudes you adopted that made it work for you?

If you find yourself thinking about the efforts of others in making your success, or you see luck as playing an important role, try to also find what *you did* that might have combined with the work of colleagues or what you did to make yourself open to take advantage of the lucky events.

What did you do, above and beyond the other factors that made a difference?

*4. If you perform a task and the outcome is not successful, identify those circumstances that prevented you from being successful. Would the result have been better if you had worked harder? Is there something you could change to improve the outcome?*

Think of a time you failed at something. What were the circumstances that led to that event being a failure for you? You will not be successful at everything, but you can find a way to learn from anything that happens.

What factors, in this unsuccessful task, were not in your control? What could you control? The next time a task like that one needs to be performed, what can you do differently so that the outcome will be better?

What do you need to learn? What do you need to practice more? What about yourself do you need to control better or control less?

*5. When you notice a weakness, remind yourself that you also have strengths. Do not define yourself by your weaknesses. Acknowledge them but also recognize that you have other positive attributes.*

When you notice that you have a weakness, you might find yourself comparing yourself to another person. If you do, it is likely that you will be comparing yourself to someone you think is better than you in that area. When human beings make comparisons with others, it is most common that the comparison is made with someone who is considered to be superior in that quality. As a result, you feel worse about yourself because of the comparison.

The most talented people are not good at everything. Those who are successful are often better at knowing what they do well and what they do not do well, and they are able to put their energy where it will have the best benefit.

You too can recognize that you are not defined by your weaknesses, and you can choose to invest energy in the parts of yourself that draw on your better skills.

*6. Find the opportunities to bring your best to every situation. You are not able to control everything that happens, but you can choose to bring the best of your talents to even the most difficult of circumstances.*

Look for the chance to contribute to a successful outcome. There are some times when an opportunity to contribute will open up that you might overlook, if you are not observant.

Sometimes the difference between success and failure is a small action done at the right time and done well. It is often an accumulation of those small actions rather than a single large effort that makes the difference.

Even when things are challenging, you can find ways to give your best rather than giving in to discouragement and giving up.

*7. Notice that the source of your happiness is grounded in what you do much more than in what you have.*

In a study done by psychologist Mihalyi Csikszentmihalyi, participants were given an electronic beeper that they carried with them throughout the day. Each time they were beeped, they recorded what they were doing and rated the level of happiness they were experiencing.

The results of this research showed that people were the happiest when they were engaged in an activity that had some meaning to them. They were happier during these activities than even during those times when they were resting or being entertained.

What you do is the greatest source of happiness for you. Choose it wisely.

*8. Approach the most difficult situations in your life as opportunities to grow and learn. Your choices, not the events, will help you define who you are.*

It is unrealistic to expect that life should always go easily or smoothly. Difficulties will arise. Things will sometimes happen that are not fair.

At these times you must make a decision about the kind of person you want to be. Will you complain about problems and surrender your happiness? Will you continue to persevere and try to be your best, even when it is hard?

These choices will shape the outcomes for your life much more than the set of events you are facing.

*9. Notice the talents and abilities of others in your life. You will bring out the best in them, and you will be practicing noticing the best in yourself.*

You might notice that there are some people in your life who are easy to be around. When you are with such a person, you feel good. You have energy. You are the best you can be.

You can be that person for others. Watch for the talents in people you encounter. When you see something good, be sure to notice it, out loud. Do it sincerely; don't say it just to say something. When it is sincere, it will be received as an authentic statement.

The person you notice will be better because of you, and you will get better at recognizing your own talents.

*10. If you believe that you have a positive contribution to make, don't be stopped by obstacles in your path. Use your skills to figure out how to overcome the obstacles.*

Encountering an obstacle does not mean you must stop. It can be a chance for you to be creative in solving a problem so that you can move forward. The history of humanity is one in which problems are encountered and overcome throughout the ages.

Treat obstacles as an opportunity to see what you can do. When your first effort is blocked, think of another way to approach it and try again.

If you believe in yourself and you persist, you will discover that you can do more that you thought you could.

What other ways have you thought about that would help you to live your life with *personal* optimism?

_____

_____

_____

_____

_____

What was your favorite tip for living your life with *personal* optimism?

_____

_____

What will you do today to live with *personal* optimism?

_____

_____

Aristotle wrote, "We are what we repeatedly do. Excellence, therefore, is not an act but a habit." One of the key attributes you demonstrate when you are an optimist is that you habitually act on your talents and apply effort to the challenges you face.

*1. Keep a journal of positive events. Good things and bad things happen every day, and you can choose where to place your attention.*

Research has shown that journaling may provide significant benefits for both mental and physical health. Research subjects who kept a journal for psychologist James Pennebaker were found to have less anxiety, less depression, and fewer visits to their physician compared to control subjects.

When you write, you focus your attention more fully on the subject of your writing. You can choose where to focus your attention. Even on days when many difficult things happen, some good things are also happening. And on days when many wonderful things occur, there will be some bad things that will take place.

By writing about the positive events of your life, you are attending to the dimensions of your life that give you happiness and joy.

*2. When you identify one of your strengths, look for opportunities to practice it every day, just like you can build your vocabulary by learning a new word and then looking for opportunities to use it.*

When my oldest granddaughter turned four, for her birthday she got her first bicycle, complete with streamers on the handles and sparkling training wheels. It was the first present she saw that year, and it was very exciting for her. As soon as every other present was open, she wanted to go out and ride her new bike.

Within a few minutes, she was showing me her new Donald Duck Band-Aid that covered the cut from her first fall.

In the meantime, her older brother (three years older) was riding his bike up and down the driveway, with no hands. How does it happen that children start learning about bike riding so tentatively and become so proficient in just a few short years?

You get good at what you practice. This is true of bike riding, expanding your vocabulary, and becoming a proficient public speaker. If you want to improve your abilities, you have to practice.

*3. If you are faced with a difficult situation, remember what you have done in the past to meet a challenge. Would that work here?*

Optimistic people succeed in situations that pessimists don't because they choose different actions in the face of trouble. One of the things that optimists do is to assume that there is a solution to a problem and to search for clues about what might work. Pessimists, by contrast, will more quickly conclude that an obstacle cannot be overcome.

You have successfully solved many problems in your life. Your past success gives you wisdom about how to deal with the present. It is a good idea to start in the problem-solving process by calling to mind what has worked before. If the situations are similar, it is a good place to start.

*4. Let go of the negative events that have happened in the past. Focus your attention on the present and the opportunities that are here now.*

When your mind gets caught up in negative thinking patterns, it can seem like your thoughts go over and over the details of those circumstances. Psychologists call that process *rumination*. Studies have shown that rumination is more strongly associated with stress-related medical problems than being depressed without ruminating.

Notice when your thoughts have fallen into rumination. Make a conscious choice to re-focus attention on the present. The present gives you opportunities to decide differently from what you did in the past.

It can be helpful to start with a mindful breath. Become aware of your physical surroundings. You might even silently describe everything you can see as you look around. Then gently but firmly direct your thoughts to the opportunities in the present moment.

*5. Give yourself credit for the effort you make, and let the outcome take care of itself. If you continue to make a positive effort, you will have more good outcomes in the long run.*

There are some things that are in your control and some things that are not. It is frustrating to attempt to force a certain outcome when you are interacting with lots of dimensions of a problem that are not in your control.

What you do control is your own action. When you consistently make a positive effort, you will sometimes succeed and sometimes fail, because your effort does not guarantee that every other factor lines up as you wish it would. The positive effort always tips the odds in your favor, though. You will get more satisfying outcomes more often than you would if you gave up.

Optimists regularly beat the odds and have more favorable outcomes because they persist in taking positive action and let the outcomes take care of themselves.

*6. Notice what you have learned from a failure you endured. Bring the lessons into the new situation you are facing now. Continue to do what was helpful and change what was not helpful.*

It seems obvious that you should try to eliminate mistakes. If you make no mistakes, you are perfect, right?

Or perhaps, if you make no mistakes, you are not trying!

New learning usually starts when you try something that you do not know how to do. In this effort to learn, you will make some mistakes.

You can react to your mistakes by being embarrassed and trying to hide them so that no one knows what you did, or you can approach the situation, recognize the mistake, and recognize the opportunity to learn from making a mistake.

It is really a failure only if you don't learn from it.

*7. When you try something and fail, do something else. When you try and succeed, try it again.*

Imagine you are watching someone working on a computer. This person types something but nothing happens on the screen. What do you think he will do next?

If he is normal, he will hit the key again. If the result is the same–still nothing happens–he will press the key several more times with great emphasis. Only after this futile effort is he likely to try something else.

Our example illustrates what happens in many areas of life. When you try something that you think should work, and it does not, you have a strong impulse to keep trying it–and to keep getting the same result.

There are times when you need to stop and try something else, but it often requires making a conscious decision.

*8. Remember life is not pass or fail. You can do something that is good and it can be done even better. You can do something that is bad, but it does not have to become catastrophic.*

When you are under stress, you have a tendency to think about events in extremes of "all or nothing." You succeed or you fail. You win or you lose.

In reality, most of life is lived in between the extremes. When you do something well, you can still dedicate your efforts to improving. Most mistakes are only mistakes and can be corrected without significant damage.

When you find yourself framing a decision as a choice between two opposite extremes, pause and see if there is a third option. (An example: Should you go to a work-related party or not? A third option might be to go for a brief time, but leave early.)

*9. Perseverance is an essential element in success. Many great accomplishments have come at the end of a long time of trying and failing but learning and trying again. Commit yourself to keep trying.*

Thomas Edison once said that he found 9,999 ways that did not work to make a light bulb before he found one way that did work.

Optimistic people tend to be more willing to persevere, even when obstacles are in the way, because they treat the barriers as opportunities to learn.

You do not have to stop because a problem is difficult to solve. Your willingness to keep trying new ways to approach a difficult barrier might yield new avenues to move forward in your life.

What problem do you need to solve today? What have you learned from the attempts you have already made that will make you more effective in your next attempt?

*10. If you were successful doing something yesterday, there is a good chance that you can be successful today by acting in a similar fashion. Keep trying the things you have found that work.*

When you discover something that works in your life, it can be useful to wonder, "Where else can I use this same approach?"

Because optimists assume that successes come from their actions and it is not just luck, they are always noticing what they did that contributed to success. They extend those successful actions to other, similar situations. This method makes it more likely that they will succeed again.

How did your actions contribute to a successful outcome in your life recently? What opportunities do you have to make similar choices in your current situation?

What other ways have you thought about that would help you live your life with *permanent* optimism?

_____

_____

_____

_____

_____

What was your favorite tip for living your life with *permanent* optimism?

_____

_____

What will you do today to live with *permanent* optimism?

_____

_____

Optimism is contagious. When you are successful in one endeavor, it makes you more confident that you can put the same hard work into being successful in other situations.

*1. Optimists are luckier than average. When you are an optimist and you happen to be in the right place at the right time, you are able to see the opportunity and therefore take steps to act on it.*

The discoveries being made by quantum physics suggest that there is a random element to all of life. Sometimes things happen that are not a result of planned action or a consequence of some mistake. A plane crashes into a residential home, killing the occupants of the home, yet those who happened to be in that home at that moment had no part in causing the tragedy.

This reality is uncomfortable. Life would be more stable if everything had a reason.

Luck is the other side of random tragedy. Sometimes something just happens that is a positive event. You did not do anything to cause it. You were in the right place at the right time. Optimists are not more likely to be in the right place at the right time. They are more likely to realize opportunity when it happens.

The loved ones of those killed in a plane crash are also victims of a horrible event that is random, but how they respond to the tragedy is a choice.

Like tragedy, luck sometimes comes along in life too. It is how you choose to deal with the luck in your life that will make the most difference.

*2. If you are stuck in a bad situation, remember that it is not a reflection of your character. Good and bad things happen all the time. You can choose how you want to respond to the difficult circumstances you face.*

There are random events, both good and bad, and they are very frequent events.

When someone says, "I am waiting for the next bad thing to happen in my life," he or she will not be disappointed. Something bad will happen.

Something good will also happen, but the person who is waiting for a bad thing to happen is more likely to notice the next bad thing than to notice the good thing that also happened.

You cannot avoid difficulties, pain, and even tragedy in your life. When it happens, it is not a punishment; it happens to everyone at some time and in some way in life. The choices you make during the challenging times of your life will make all the difference.

*3. If you are able to use a strength to accomplish something, look for other opportunities to continue to use that strength.*

You were born with a set of abilities. As you grew and discovered what some of these abilities were, you practiced and learned about these abilities, and they became skills.

When a skill matches the demands of an environment, you are able to have a positive impact on the task at hand. If you are able to apply that skill often, it becomes a strength.

For example, if you have a strength as a good communicator, look for chances to use that skill. Volunteer for tasks that give you a chance to help by communicating well. When you notice any skill, use it whenever you have the opportunity.

*4. You will not know what you can do until you try. You are probably capable of more than you realize. Recognize that the thought, "I can't" is just a thought.*

It is easy to limit your life by not trying new things. If you never risk, you will not fail. But if you never risk, you will not find out what you are able to do.

What have you always wanted to try? What has kept you from acting on that desire? Is there an opportunity to try it now?

If what holds you back is self-doubt, you might be able to do more than you think you can. You will never know unless you try.

*5. Look at a new situation as an opportunity to have a new experience rather than as the need to prove your self worth. If you always need to prove yourself, you won't try things unless you are sure you can succeed. As a result, you will miss out on many chances to experience joy.*

Looking at something as an opportunity to have a new experience is quite different from seeing it as a need to prove yourself.

In the first attitude, you are open to enjoyment and looking forward to what is unfolding in the moment.

In the second attitude, you are defending yourself and trying to keep yourself safe from the disapproving stance of other people. You are trying to avoid embarrassment.

Joy in life comes from approaching what is happening. It comes from actively choosing to participate in the events of your life. Taking the attitude of *approach* will broaden and build good things in your life.

*6. Challenge yourself to try something new each day. Continuous learning is good for your brain health and good for your emotional health.*

If you want more joy in life, look for opportunities to try something new each day. It does not need to be something of great significance. For example, it might include learning a new fact or tasting a new food.

The joy you see in little children arises from their curiosity about the world. There are lots of opportunities for experiencing something new if you are a child.

There are also lots of opportunities for experiencing something new if you are an adult.

*7. Even if you think you cannot perform some activity, remember that it is only your opinion. You might surprise yourself if you are willing to approach it as something you can learn rather than holding to the belief that you either have the ability to do it or you don't.*

You need a great deal of talent to become a professional athlete or a star performer in the theater. You also need a lot of coaching and thousands of hours of practice.

Human beings start out unable to do much for themselves. They must learn everything. Newborn babies must learn to control muscles to raise their heads and then to turn over. Toddlers must learn to walk and acquire words that will allow them to communicate.

You are capable of learning many things, if you have the right mindset. Even in areas where you are the expert, you are capable of learning more and expanding your skills.

*8. Resist the urge to label yourself or your abilities. Labels are limiting when you see the label as a description that prevents you from experiencing an event as it unfolds.*

A few years ago, I was on a vacation at a beach on the Gulf of Mexico. As evening fell, there were small pockets of clouds and rain over the Gulf. Suddenly, just about fifty yards off the shoreline, a small waterspout rose out of the surf. The spout, created by a swirling wind current, followed the shoreline as it moved from north to south.

It moved parallel to a man who was walking the beach. He was on his cell phone, and he never once looked up to see the very unusual event. It seemed as if the man had walked the beach so often, he no longer bothered to look around to see what might be happening.

You also might risk missing extraordinary experiences if you become too complacent and think you know all about something in your life.

Just for a moment, let go of the label and really see, hear, taste, smell, or touch something in your life.

*9. When others doubt your abilities, treat their statements as an opinion and not as a fact. There are many opinions, and not all of them will be true.*

You have learned to accept your abilities and talents. You have begun to cultivate an attitude of openness and curiosity about your life. But there are still people who will tell you that you are not good enough.

The people who point out your limitations do so for a number of reasons. It may be out of concern for you, or it may be a way that the individual is trying to make you feel bad about your ability.

In either case, this person may be wrong.

Treat the statements you hear about your ability as opinions, not as facts. It is not more likely that another person will know you better than you know yourself. You needed to test your beliefs to determine if they were realistic. Test the beliefs you hear from others, too, before you act as if they are true.

*10. Each night before going to sleep, take some time and acknowledge what you have done well. By recognizing your abilities, you will become more aware of your skills as you engage in the new day to come.*

The end of the day is a natural time to pause and think back. You can foster good sleep habits and wake up more refreshed if you use that pause to consider the times during the day you have acted positively.

You may find yourself prone to thinking back through the day and reliving all the "mistakes" you think you made. You might toss and turn, worrying about what will happen tomorrow.

Or you could make a different choice. Try calling to mind the things you did well and let yourself acknowledge the positive things in your life. You can give energy to your mistakes or to your successes. You will get lasting benefits from paying attention to your good actions.

What other ways have you thought about that help you live your life with *pervasive* optimism?

_____

_____

_____

_____

_____

What was your favorite tip for living your life with *pervasive* optimism?

_____

_____

What will you do today to live with *pervasive* optimism?

_____

_____

# RESILIENCE

*Obstacles don't have to stop you.*
*If you run into a wall, don't turn around and give up.*
*Figure out how to climb it, go through it,*
*or work around it.*
*- Michael Jordan*

# REſILIENCE

Two psychologists at the University of Chicago, Salvador Maddi and Diane Khoshaba, asked an interesting question in the early 1980s when they were studying a large organization that was undergoing a major downsizing.

"What is different about those individuals who endure this difficult time and who *stay healthy*?"

They knew that stress and massive changes cause a significant increase in both physical and mental problems. They also knew that there would be a drop in performance following the traumatic event.

They found a group of individuals who did not get sick, either physically or emotionally, and who actually increased performance during the stressful time. They studied the qualities that these workers possessed that allowed them to be resilient.

You might think of these qualities as analogous to taking a daily dose of vitamins. They are qualities that help you resist the negative effects of stress.

There are three "Vitamin C's" of a resilient life. When you cultivate the recommended dose of these "Vitamin C's" the resilience of your day-to-day living improves. The C's are as follows:

commitment,
challenge, and
control.

# COMMITMENT

David Whyte, poet and organizational consultant, says, "Anything or anyone that does not bring you alive is too small." The first vitamin C of resilience is commitment. You need to work for something that is larger than yourself. When you have an articulated purpose that contributes to making the world a better place, you will be better able to commit time and energy to your life.

*1. Develop a clear personal mission statement and post it where you will see it. It is a written identification of your most important values. It reminds you of how you want to live your life.*

There is something about writing that clarifies thought and makes intentions more possible to achieve. Organizations have realized this fact, and successful organizations have set aside time to construct and display a mission statement. You can create a similar document for your personal mission.

An effective mission statement identifies the values you hold most important in your life. It clarifies the central goals you have and helps you organize your decisions.

What do you want your life to mean? How do you want to take action to get where you are going? These are the questions that a good mission statement addresses.

*2. Keep in mind the "big picture" for your life. It is easy to get lost in the annoying but often trivial problems in the workplace or at home. The big picture helps you maintain perspective.*

It is difficult to make good decisions during the stresses and strains of daily life. You find yourself shouting at the kids for things that are unimportant. You react to the political tensions at work and do something you later regret.

Small decisions can have large consequences. It is important to make choices with the "big picture" of your life in mind.

When you act this way, will you be living in a way that matches the deepest values you hold? Are you willing to let go of an immediate pleasure if it will mean a positive long-term outcome?

Take a (metaphorical) step back from your life and make sure you are living it as your best self.

*3. Communicate your purpose to others around you. Let them know what is important to you. Once you do, you will find that you hold yourself accountable, because you don't want to disappoint them.*

If you let others know what you really believe, they might look at how you act and think you are a hypocrite because you fall short of what you want to be. One solution is to keep silent about your values, so that no one will be disappointed in you.

Another solution is to be clear about what you believe and make more effort to translate it into action.

You might even consider asking a close friend if he or she would be willing to hold you accountable, so you can be living the kind of life you really want to live.

*4. Discuss your values and how they contribute to your family, your work, and to the human community. Values become effective only when they are translated into actions.*

Thinking about values can be a very abstract exercise. It takes effort to translate values into practical actions.

Start by identifying a value. How would it look if you lived according to this value when you are with your family? What would you do at work if you were true to what you believe? Are there implications for your role in the greater society?

Repeat this process for each of your important values. At the end of the day, review your behavior to see if your intentions matched your actions.

*5. Stand for something important and encourage others in around you to do the same. Commitment is contagious.*

It may seem as though it does not matter if you take a stand for something that you believe is right. Others who are more powerful or more influential might oppose you.

Your actions speak to those who love you and look up to you, though. You have friends who might believe just as strongly as you, but they do not speak up or do something, because it seems they would be a single voice. Your willingness to take action will help them to find the courage to do what they can do, too.

You might ask yourself, "Why should I be the one to do it?"

You could also ask, "Why not me?"

*6. Discuss the value you offer your coworkers and loved ones. It is not bragging. Your willingness to talk about the service you offer may inspire others to do the same.*

You can remember times when a group of coworkers or friends were gathered and everyone was complaining about something. You probably joined in. Conversations like that can affect the mood of everyone involved.

What would happen if you started a different conversation? What if you began to talk about your decisions to be of help to others? Would this action bring about a different discussion? Would it bring about a different mood? Would others be willing to join in?

What emotional tone would this kind of conversation elicit?

*7. Make long-term outcomes more important than short-term financial benefits. Commitment involves action over a lifetime.*

The date tree is a popular tree in the Middle East. It yields a sweet fruit and offers a shady place in an often hot and dry landscape. If you plant a date tree, you will not enjoy it. Your children will not get usefulness from it. It will begin to bear fruit for your grandchildren.

Like planters of the date tree, resilient individuals take the long view. The ups and downs of the present are looked at in the perspective of a bigger picture. The short-term decisions support the overall goals.

What are the goals you have in your life? What decisions are you making today that will help you achieve those long-term objectives?

*8. Discuss values openly and non-judgmentally. You don't need to argue with others about your values. Others will be convinced of your commitment by how you live more than by what you say.*

Sometimes you encounter a person who seems intent on convincing you of his or her point of view. How often are you persuaded by an argument presented like this? How often do you find yourself agreeing on points that you already accept and resisting where you disagreed at the outset?

Presenting a logical argument usually does not change your mind about values. Making your case will not change the mind of someone else.

You will be persuasive when you "walk the talk." If you are living in accord with your values, day in and day out, you will convince others that you are authentic.

*9. Listen to the ideas of others, including others with whom you agree and disagree. Your life will be enriched whenever you understand others better.*

It is comfortable to be around others who share your point of view. Communication is easier. You feel accepted for your ideas. You are reinforced in what you value.

It is more challenging to engage in real conversation with a person who has different ideas. Listen to what the person has to say, as openly as you are able. Try to understand, even if you disagree, how he or she came to that position.

Learning in this way can be uncomfortable. At the same time, it is a way of expanding to appreciate the vast diversity of the world in which you live.

*10. Take the needs of others as serious as your own needs. This is a challenge because it involves balancing two important values. Do not give in to thinking about this as either/or; both your needs and the needs of others are important.*

Either/or thinking is characteristic of thinking that occurs when you are under stress. Either you fight or you flee. Either you survive or you perish.

Resilient thinking is more inclusive. You can value *both* quiet time *and* time with those you love. You can *both* be productive in your work *and* take time to relax. You can *both* make your children important *and* be willing to care for your own needs.

Where do you act as if you must make an *either/or* choice in your daily life? Can you approach it from the perspective of a *both/and* choice?

What other ways have you thought about that would help you live your life with commitment?

_____

_____

_____

_____

_____

What was your favorite tip for living your life with commitment?

_____

_____

What will you do today to live with commitment?

_____

_____

The Chinese character for *crisis* can be translated
two ways, either as a problem or an opportunity.
The powerful truth is that for success, optimism and
the willingness to persevere are more important than
intelligence or skill. When you foster the sense of
challenge you bring out the best you have to offer.
The second vitamin C fosters a challenging
environment.

*1. Change your inner language to think of opportunities rather than problems. By reminding yourself to look for the opportunities, you will be more successful in finding solutions to the challenges you are facing.*

The most successful people in life have a "Plan B." No matter how good you are at planning for life's circumstances, you will find that your plan will not always work. Obstacles are normal. Unanticipated intrusions into life happen with great frequency.

Resilience allows you to meet these problems with a different positive attitude. Rather than complaining, when you are resilient, you recognize every roadblock as an opportunity to learn something and to explore the challenges you face in new ways.

Try to adopt a mindset that is solution focused. Not everything you plan will work out as you planned it. Prepare a "Plan B" and keep looking for the way through.

*2. Persevere when projects are important even when the answers are elusive. Thomas Edison said, "Creativity is one percent inspiration and ninety-nine percent perspiration."*

Most new and great innovations, big and small, are actually the result of very hard work to make an idea work.

When you feel paralyzed about what decision to make, remember that you will not always be able to achieve certainty before you make a choice. It is important to do your best to think things through and look at the benefits and the consequences of important decisions, but the work does not end there.

You must make a decision, and then you begin the more important process of making that decision work.

*3. Promote optimistic attitudes in your daily life. Remind yourself that you can do a great deal when you put your mind to it.*

Resilient people do not expect that life will always be smooth or that everything will work out in the end. Resilient people have cultivated confidence that their efforts will be an important component of the effort to live in a stressful life circumstance.

You are able to do more than you may think. Most of the time, life does not require that you give the extra effort, but some of the time it does.

When you are in a challenging situation, it is useful to distinguish between things that are hard to do and things that you cannot do.

When you say to yourself, "This is hard," you can also remind yourself, "I have done hard things before. I can do it."

*4. Identify your strengths and learn to use them effectively. You have talents and skills that you bring to the job at hand. If you know your strengths and use them, you will bring the best of yourself to the task.*

When you are in a challenging situation, start by identifying your personal strengths. See if any of these strengths might be useful in dealing with the current circumstances.

When you start by complaining, being afraid, or feeling overwhelmed, it can use up all your energy.

Start instead by doing a quick self-analysis. Look for your personal qualities that might serve as resources. You will be more successful if you bring your best to the problems at hand.

*5. Take advantage of advanced training opportunities. Learn more about what you do well and become excellent in your area of expertise.*

Whatever you are good at doing, you can get even better at doing it. You will find that learning about something you do well is interesting and engaging. It is learning that will become practical because you will discover ways of integrating it into things you are doing every day.

Dedicate yourself to being really good at something in your life. Become the expert. Pursue at least one passion in your life.

*6. Cultivate positive goal setting. It is easier to identify what you want to stop doing than what you want to start, but it is a better guide to articulate where you want to go in your life.*

When you set a goal, identify it as something that is positive. It should be something that you want to approach.

Painful realities sometimes intrude in your life, and your impulse is to find a way to get rid of the pain. Take the additional step of clearly defining what you would want instead.

Here are a few questions to ask yourself in this process:

- How will my life be different when this problem is resolved?
- How will I know when I get to that different life?
- What is the smallest change I will notice that tells me I am moving in the right direction?
- What can I do today to get started?

*7. Engage in continuous learning. Keeping your brain active is good for the physical health of your brain, but it is also an effective way to keep life interesting. What have you always wanted to learn more about? What keeps you from learning more about it today?*

You graduated from school. The graduation ceremony implies that school has been completed and you are ready to move on to a new phase of your life.

It can be misleading if you associate school with learning, because learning does not come to an end when schooling ends.

It is healthy for your brain to keep learning, in the same way that it is healthy for your body to keep exercising. You can keep life interesting and fun by recognizing that there are opportunities to learn new things daily.

Find something to learn today.

*8. Be willing to attempt to solve problems, even if you make mistakes along the way. You can learn as much from your mistakes as from your successes, if you pay attention.*

Psychologist Ellen Langer does an exercise where she goes into an elementary school classroom and asks the students to draw a picture of morning. About halfway through the drawing she stops the children and tells them she made a mistake. She did not mean for them to draw a picture of morning as a time of the day, but a picture of mourning as an emotion that happens when you lose something important.

"But," she says, "don't start over, just include this emotion in whatever picture you were already drawing."

The children are able to easily incorporate the "mistake" into the drawing, and the result is a much more thoughtful and insightful depiction of the human emotion of mourning.

You encounter situations that are not what they seemed when you started. Can you find a way to continue and to integrate the "mistake" into what you are doing?

*9. Encourage creativity and the willingness to take risks. When you impose a standard of perfection on your actions, you will be less willing to try things that you can't be perfect doing, which only limits you.*

Children are naturally creative. They love to draw, build things, and make things. It does not matter that the finished product does not meet someone's standards. The process itself brings joy to the child doing the work.

As you grow up, something changes. You become worried about the outcome of your efforts. You compare what you do with what someone else does. (Most people compare themselves to someone they consider to be better in that skill, so the comparison leads to feeling inadequate.) Because of a concern over the outcome, some of us find it harder to engage in creative activities.

Take a risk again. Be creative. Enjoy the process. Let it be about the act of creating and not about the end results.

*10. Work on resolving problems. Obstacles are only problems to be solved, not a reason to give up.*

You will sometimes be discouraged. It can be difficult to keep trying, day after day, when there are problems and obstacles in the way. It is not always obvious how to move forward or whether a problem is able to be resolved.

This problem is not unique to you. It is a problem that everyone faces.

Developing skills in resilience include skills in being able to keep going in the face of disappointment and discouragement. The feeling of distress is not the thing that will stop you. Giving up will be the only thing that stops you.

What other ways have you thought about that would help you live your life with challenge?

_____

_____

_____

_____

_____

What was your favorite tip for living your life with challenge?

_____

_____

What will you do today to live with challenge?

_____

_____

# CONTROL

It's important to be able to choose situations in your daily life in order to be more effective and use your skills, because having control reduces the stress you experience. The third vitamin C is control. Establishing a sense of control is a key factor in reducing stress and in increasing productivity.

*1. When accepting responsibility for a job, make sure you also have the authority to carry it out. You can endure even the most difficult task when you know you have the capability to accomplish your goal.*

When researchers studied the effects of stress at work they discovered that executives at large companies actually were among those who were least likely to suffer from stress-related problems. Employees were more likely to have problems with physical and psychological abnormalities.

Those most likely to be affected by stress, however, were those in the middle management of the organization. Individuals at these levels were likely to be given high levels of responsibility, but frequently did not have the authority to make changes.

Make sure you have the ability to make things work if you accept responsibility for a task. It is best to discuss this point at the very beginning of the job.

*2. Identify what is in your control and work within your circle of influence. Some things are not in your control. Other things fall within your control, or at least under your influence. Put your energy on those things.*

There is a fable about a princess who went for a walk outside the castle. As she walked, she stepped on a sharp stone and cut her foot. The angry princess demanded that the king cover the whole kingdom in leather so that she would never step on a sharp stone again.

The princess in this story wasted her energy trying to control things that were not in her control. She needed only to put shoes on her own feet to resolve her troubles.

Are there times when you waste energy trying to control the actions of others when you would be more successful making a change in yourself?

*3. There are many ways to accomplish a task. If one approach to accomplishing your task is blocked, look for a different way to proceed.*

Resilient people are flexible in solving problems. Sometimes something that "should" work does not. It is not a matter of trying harder. Complaining that it is *not fair* and it *should* work does not result in a better outcome.

Use the energy more wisely. When a particular way of solving a problem does not work–even if it should work–shift your efforts to a different way of doing things.

The willingness to experiment with a new approach might also yield a new way of understanding something.

*4. Assume responsibility for your own behavior. Avoid blaming others for your mistakes. You won't change behavior if you believe you are not responsible. Taking responsibility is the key to growth.*

Change is hard. It is not easy to make choices that are different from the ones you have made all your life. It is fair to say that important changes in life do not happen by accident.

If you want to change, you must start by taking responsibility for what you want to change. As long as you believe that the problem is in the other person, or that you are a victim of circumstances, you will be frustrated in your efforts to make the changes you want.

When you acknowledge the role you play in your distress, you will see clearly what you can do to make it better.

*5. Be flexible. When one door closes in your life, look for another door that opens. If you remain flexible, you might find opportunities you did not know about.*

Not everything works out the way you hoped. Things happen that cause us to suffer losses.

If you choose to focus on what you have lost, you are unable to move forward in your life. Focusing on your loss may be important to do for a period of time as you grieve.

But when you are ready to move on, you must change your focus. Look for new possibilities that may offer themselves to you in the situation. You will see them only if you are looking for them.

*6. Give yourself time to plan and organize. It can seem as though you do not have time to plan, but when you are organized, you will be more efficient and effective.*

The pressures of modern life can be extreme. It seems as if you are spending all your time dealing with crisis after crisis. You begin to feel reactive. There is time to deal with only whatever is most painful, most intrusive at the moment.

Although it seems counterintuitive, this is the time to make some space for planning and organizing. The pressure of constant reaction is an inefficient and ineffective way to work in a crisis.

Making time to plan and organize will give you a better chance to address the issues in a more satisfying manner.

*7. Accept input from others about the best way to do your job. When you are working with a team, ask your teammates for their ideas about their work too.*

Humans are social creatures. You can do more and do it more effectively when you work with a team. It can be a work group, family members, friends working on a project, or it can take many other forms.

Teamwork involves communicating about the task at hand and also communicating about the relationships among team members.

Ask team members to give you feedback about how you are doing. Listen with an open mind to what they say. Keep the channels of communication open.

*8. Balance your work life with your family life and your leisure. All aspects of your life are important. You will be most effective when you tend to each aspect.*

You are probably finding it easier to stay in constant touch with others these days. With that amount of communication can come greater demands, at work or with friends and family members. It can seem as though you must always be available.

Let go of this form of "all or nothing" thinking. Life is meant to be lived in a balanced way. There is a time for work and a time for relaxation. There is a time to interact socially with others and a time to be alone.

It is important to maintain balance for yourself. Burnout primarily comes from getting out of balance and not making choices that keep things in perspective.

*9. Acquire information essential to your work. If you are going to do the best you can, you need to be serious about learning all you are able to learn about the work you are doing (including learning more about being in a relationship or about being a parent).*

What work is most important to you? Is it your job? Is it your relationship with your partner? Is it your role as a parent?

Whatever your work, you have the opportunity to learn and grow in your ability. Take it as a solemn responsibility. Become the best at your work that you can.

Self-improvement may include reading, attending classes, or studying with a small group of close friends.

You expect your doctor to keep up on his or her profession. You want the best from your pastor. Hold the same expectations for your own work.

*10. Make sure you have the material supplies you need to do your work. You will benefit from clarifying what is most important in your life and committing your material resources to reflect your values.*

There are many competing demands for your attention. There are products for nearly every need you can imagine, and some for things in life that are not needs, yet there are also limited resources.

You must make decisions about where to put your energy and about where to use your money. Take time to understand what is most important to you when you are considering what material goods you need.

Your life will be happier if your material possessions are a reflection of the values that are most important to you.

What other ways have you thought about that would help you live your life with control?

_____

_____

_____

_____

_____

What was your favorite tip for living your life with control?

_____

_____

What will you do today to live with control?

_____

_____

# DEPRESSION FACTS

*Let us not look back in anger or forward in fear but around in awareness.*

*- James Thurber*

# DEPRESSION FACTS

- ✓ Two thirds of both men and women say that work has a significant impact on their stress level, and one in four has called in sick or taken a "mental-health day" as a result of work stress. (American Psychological Association, 2004)

- ✓ Problems at work are more strongly associated with health complaints than any other life stressor. (St. Paul Co.)

- ✓ Health insurance premiums have increased at a rate more than three times the growth in workers' earnings and two-and-a-half times the rate of inflation. (Kaiser Family Foundation, 2005)

- ✓ Sixty-two percent of Americans said their workload has increased in the past six months and that they had not used all their allotted vacation time in the past year. (Kronos Inc., 2004)

- ✓ American employees used about 8.8 million sick days in 2001 because of untreated or mistreated depression. (National Committee for Quality Assurance, 2004)

- ✓ Depression results in more days of disability than chronic health conditions such as heart disease, hypertension, and diabetes. (National Committee for Quality Assurance, 2004)

- ✓ According to the National Institutes of Mental Health, depression costs an estimated $23 billion in lost workdays each year.

# CONCLUDING THOUGHTS

When I was in training to become a psychologist, I assumed I would be working with people who encountered a problem while living a normal, fulfilling life. Our work together would be aimed at resolving that problem and, once the problem was gone, life would again be happy.

Instead, I encounter people who are living difficult and stressful lives with only brief pockets of calm and happiness. This reality is the opposite of my earlier assumption.

Alleviating a current problem sometimes has little effect, because there are larger problems: life is too stressful, too difficult, and enjoyment is the exception rather than the rule.

It is necessary, then, to make more fundamental changes–changes in the way you think–to bring about the true peace of mind that was considered to be normal.

Learning healthy thinking skills is an important element in creating a good quality of life for yourself. Along with other healthy habits, you can create a life that is open to growth and flourishes with possibilities. It will take work, skill, and persistence, but a satisfying life is possible!

# RECOMMENDED READING

*Authentic Happiness: Using the New Positive Psychology to Realize Your Potential for Lasting Fulfillment* by Martin Seligman

*Learned Optimism: How to Change Your Mind and Your Life* by Martin Seligman

*Lifting Depression* by Kelly Lambert

*The Mindful Way Through Depression: Freeing Yourself from Chronic Unhappiness* by Mark Williams, John Teasdale, Zindel Segal, and Jon Kabat-Zinn

*Resilience at Work: How to Succeed No Matter What Life Throws at You* by Salvatore Maddi and Deborah Khoshaba

*The Resilience Factor: 7 Keys to Finding Your Inner Strength and Overcoming Life's Hurdles* by Karen Reivich and Andrew Shatte

*Train Your Mind, Change Your Brain* by Sharon Begley

*Wherever You Go, There You Are* by Jon Kabat-Zinn

**The Healthy Thinking Initiative**

# Get M.O.R.E. out of life...

Mindfulness
Optimism
Resilience
Experience the difference.

## www.healthythinkinginitiative.com

Take advantage of our comprehensive program for the prevention of anxiety and depression in your workplace. The program includes the following:

- *Mental Health Risk Assessments* for the identification of anxiety- and depression-related problems in your organization

- Training in three key skills of *mindfulness, optimism,* and *resilience* conducted by our experienced professional staff

- Supportive written materials to ensure that the skills we teach can be used in the day-to-day world of work.

Your benefits?

Measurable Results:
*Reduced Absenteeism!*
*Lower healthcare costs!*

We are committed to bringing you the highest quality program that is available. Programs are available onsite or online in a real-time, interactive format. Call today to arrange a free consultation.
**(262) 544-6486**

**John Weaver, Psy.D.** is a licensed psychologist who received his Doctor of Psychology degree from the Wisconsin School of Professional Psychology. He also has a Master of Science degree in Clinical Psychology from Marquette University and a Master of Divinity degree from St. Francis School of Pastoral Ministry.

John is the director of **The Healthy Thinking Initiative** and has coordinated the efforts of the development team. He has taught mindfulness to groups and individuals since 1997 and has been engaged in his own mindfulness work since 1972. He works both as a clinical psychologist and a business consultant with more than twenty years of practical experience with organizations, individuals, and groups. He is the author of nine articles for business publications, including "Surviving Real World Stress," "Remedies for Workplace Violence," and "Failures of a 'Perfect' Leader," and he is cofounder and owner of **Psychology for Business**, bringing applied psychology to business and industry. He is the chair of the Wisconsin Psychological Association Psychologically Healthy Workplace Award committee and is an accomplished professional speaker.

You can contact Dr. Weaver to speak at your next conference or to arrange a consultation with him by phone: (262) 544-6486 or by e-mail: jweaver@preventingdepression.com. Visit the Healthy Thinking Initiative Web site: http://www.preventingdepression.com.

Printed in the United States
151217LV00004B/5/P